Understanding the U.S. Government: A Guide to Understanding American Government and Elections

Authored by

Peter E. Tarlow

&

Stephen H. Vincent

Understanding the U.S. Government:
A Guide to Understanding American Government and Elections

Authors: Peter E. Tarlow and Stephen H. Vincent

ISBN (Online): 978-981-5274-07-3

ISBN (Print): 978-981-5274-08-0

ISBN (Paperback): 978-981-5274-09-7

need for a court order if at any point you breach any terms of this License Agreement. In no event will any delay or failure by Bentham Science Publishers in enforcing your compliance with this License Agreement constitute a waiver of any of its rights.

3. You acknowledge that you have read this License Agreement, and agree to be bound by its terms and conditions. To the extent that any other terms and conditions presented on any website of Bentham Science Publishers conflict with, or are inconsistent with, the terms and conditions set out in this License Agreement, you acknowledge that the terms and conditions set out in this License Agreement shall prevail.

Bentham Science Publishers Pte. Ltd.
80 Robinson Road #02-00
Singapore 068898
Singapore
Email: subscriptions@benthamscience.net

BENTHAM SCIENCE

CONTENTS

FOREWORD

Every book is a journey. When I first open a new one, I like to scan the table of contents to get a feel of where the authors are trying to take me. When I opened *Understanding the U.S. Government: A Guide to Understanding American Government and Elections* and skimmed the table of contents, I must admit I began to sweat a little. The series of questions that Peter Tarlow and Stephen Vincent have used to frame this book instantly transported me back to the final exam of my high school civics class, which is not one of my prouder moments. Luckily, unlike that inconsiderate final exam, after raising my blood pressure with those questions, they gave me the answers!

This book is a wonderful reminder of things that are inspirational, confusing, mysterious, frustrating, and practical in our system of governance. More importantly, it is a great primer on how we as citizens can and should participate in that system. It reminds us that, in a successful democracy, "leaders are encouraged to do the will of the people". Of course, that only works if those leaders know the will of the people. Our job is to tell them. And each of us, no matter where we sit on the political spectrum or how active we have been in our democracy up to this point, has the right and the privilege of making a crystal-clear statement with our vote.

I still remember the first year I voted. I asked myself a lot of the questions that are in the table of contents of this book. I felt stupid because I didn't already know the answers, and I didn't want to embarrass myself by asking someone. I would have loved to have this book available back then. It would have removed so many of the artificial concerns and self-doubts that kept me from fully embracing my ability as a citizen to make a difference in this country.

Shortly after I cast my first vote in a presidential election, I entered the United States Air Force. I spent the next 40 years trying to remain as apolitical as possible in my professional life. When I retired, I became the dean of a graduate school founded on the idea of public service as a noble calling, on the criticality of being part of the public solution, and on the imperative of serving your fellow citizens. Reading this book made me realize I had forgotten the answers to many of the questions the authors have addressed. It reminded me that "elections have consequences" and that the role ordinary citizens play in our democracy is the cornerstone of that democracy. It reminded me that the role I play matters. And it gave me knowledge that I need to play that role more capably in the future. I am confident it will do the same for you.

Every book is a journey…this one leads to a better America.

General (Ret.) Mark A. Welsh III
Texas A&M University
20th Chief of Staff, Air Force, United States

ABSTRACT

This book provides a practical overview of the mechanics and philosophical underpinnings of the United States political system, which has been quite successful for over two centuries. It is a handbook or guide for American citizens to generate more informed decisions and for people from other lands to understand this system that impacts the entire world.

Questions and answers discuss the United States' founding documents, the mechanics of the American election system, and the differences between local, state, and federal governments. Explorations include how money and political contributions, through lobbyists, individual donations, and PACs, impact the United States and its political decisions.

CHAPTER 1

The Preface

In 2019, Peter Tarlow and Steve Vincent decided to write a book explaining in layperson's terms how the United States of America's elections work. That book was written by Americans, for Americans. The book's goal was to become a valuable tool for American voters and soon-to-be voters. That 2019 book is the inspiration for this current book.

Tarlow and Vincent did not set out to author a detailed academic book, but this book aims to provide basic information to help Americans become knowledgeable citizens.

Although this book speaks directly to an American audience, it also aims to provide insights into the American political system for those who observe it from afar and often need clarification on the workings of the American political and election system.

This book is presented in a classical "question and answer" style for ease of understanding. The questions asked in this book— and the answers provided—will help you decide what you consider essential for the country, and they will give you the tools that you can use to be involved in the direction of our nation's future. We have tried to focus on the fundamental questions and answers that every citizen needs. We encourage you to foster further questions.

Anyone who follows the news knows that people can be extremely passionate about politics. This book attempts to stay at arm's length from these heated debates. Instead, it provides basic factual information for anyone wanting to understand the American political process. We use examples from the past to give clarity to issues. Our intention is not to invoke emotion.

You will find an appendix at the end of the book through which you can enhance your knowledge.

The United States' system of government is Built upon the concept of what works and what does not work in governance. It is complicated, cumbersome, imperfect, and under constant scrutiny and modification. But it has been effective in producing one of history's great countries.

We hope this book will inspire in you a veracious appetite to better understand and become involved in the grand experiment called American Democracy.

CHAPTER 2

Maintaining Personal Relations in an Age of Political Discord

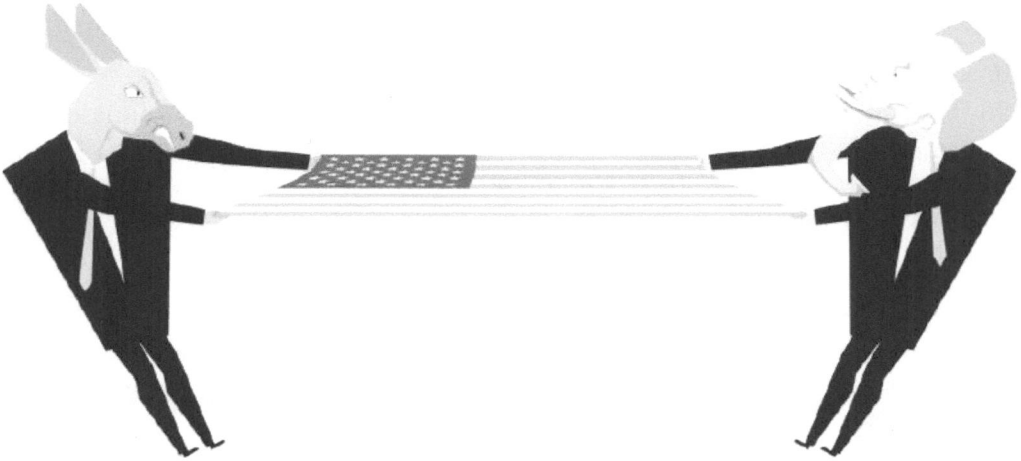

Keywords: Political discord, Political intimidation.

Once upon a time, people in polite company did not discuss money, politics, and religion. People with good manners did not discuss these subjects during family get-togethers or when socializing, networking, or celebrating. Today, only a few people follow this unwritten social rule. Not only do we discuss money, politics, and religion, but these topics have almost turned into contact sports.

Most people still firmly believe that when playing a sport, the players must follow the rules. There is a winner and a loser, and at the end of the match, everyone comes together, shakes hands, and tries to learn from their mistakes. Unfortunately, we now live in an age where the "game" of politics never ends, and the losing side does not recognize that the other team has won. Furthermore, too many people judge other people by their political views. We have become opposing rivals instead of just having opposing ideas.

Peter E. Tarlow and Stephen H. Vincent

HOW DO I MAINTAIN A RELATIONSHIP WITH PEOPLE WITH WHOM I DISAGREE?

So, how do we keep our relationships with those we love? If possible, avoid the conversation or refuse to answer. At least two people are required to fight, but if you do not engage, there is no argument.

Avoidance, however, will not always work. When it fails, hold your ground and consider some of the following suggestions. Remember, that in an age of hypersensitivity and overreaction, there are no magic solutions.

- Smile! No matter how the other person tries to provoke you, smile and use a loving tone.
- Listen and be respectful to someone you disagree with and insist that the other person do the same.
- Speak in a low, calm voice.
- Know when to hear and when to ignore snide remarks.
- Remind the provoker that people have the right to disagree.
- Emphasize that we all want what is best for our country; we have different roads to achieve the same goals.
- Smile! Smile! Then smile some more.
- End with something like, "Even though we disagree, I love you" or "You are my friend."

HOW DO I SURVIVE WHEN EVERYONE IS SO SURE THEIR OPINION IS THE ONLY CORRECT OPINION?

The news is full of people mocking, screaming, and insulting one another all because they are sure that only their own opinions are correct, and give the impression that anyone who has a different view should be sent to re-education camps or done away with. Sometimes, we wonder whether some people's sole purpose is to post ridiculousness on social media to make their family and future "former friends" hate them. These people's minds are made up, and no quantity of facts can change their opinion. Hopefully, these extreme people do not represent most Americans. In this case, the easiest solution is to avoid these people.

The best way to survive is to refuse to be drawn into yelling matches or purely emotional arguments. Instead, educate yourself about the actions governments take and the policies they enact to make this a better country. Most of us hope that our country will benefit all its citizens. However, not all governmental actions are good. Governments are composed of human beings. At all levels of government, there are times when people make mistakes, or their actions or decisions are later judged to be shameful.

We are aware that all governments have, at times, failed their citizens. Governments are composed of people who sometimes lie, do things that harm rather than help, carry out actions for their benefit, or make simple unintentional errors. Some politicians lie. Some politicians seek office for their benefit rather than for the good of the people they represent. There are others that history has shown were wrong. These lies are like the wolf dressed in sheep's clothing. These selfish and self-serving politicians benefit the few to the detriment of the many.

HOW DO I KEEP FROM BEING INTIMIDATED?

Be strong in your beliefs, be steadfast, and be polite. Never be belligerent. Giving in to bullies only encourages them to continue to bully you or others. If you have a valuable relationship with an intimidator, then try to avoid the topic. If that does not work, then be polite but stand your ground.

SHOULD I GO TO PROTESTS OR RALLIES? HOW EFFECTIVE ARE THEY?

It depends on how strongly you feel about a topic. Gatherings are important in that they express a group's position, and there is strength in numbers.

Some political rallies have been highly effective. The fight to end segregation was highly successful. Often, the success of a protest depends on interworking the protest with media coverage and how often the protest occurs. Ideally, protests with a righteous cause will be the most successful. Single protest rallies rarely do much; continual and well-orchestrated protests can do a lot. In the past, political rallies were thought to have little impact, but President Trump has turned this notion on its head and successfully used rallies to go around the media and speak directly to the citizens, thus inspiring his followers.

CHAPTER 3

Rights and Responsibilities

Keywords: Civil rights, Civic duties, Human rights.

WHAT ARE THE DIFFERENCES BETWEEN HUMAN RIGHTS, CIVIL RIGHTS, AND CIVIC DUTIES?

Human rights are generally viewed as fundamental rights that transcend national boundaries. In 1948, in response to the Holocaust perpetrated by German Nazis, the United Nations General Assembly adopted the *Universal Declaration of Human Rights* as a foundation of international law. These principles are based on, and expanded from, *Les doits de l'homme et du citroyen* (translated into English as *the Declaration of the Rights of Man* by the Yale Law School Avalon Project) during the French Revolution. The document was promulgated on August 26, 1789. These rights were meant to guarantee the right to life and protection from torture.

The term "Civil Rights", as differentiated from human rights, refers to the rights that one has by being a citizen of a specific nation, in this case, being a citizen of the United States.

Below, you will find some of the rights that all United States citizens have and which the government is obliged to respect.

- Freedom to express yourself.
- Freedom to worship as you wish.
- Right to a prompt, fair trial by jury.
- Right to vote in elections for public officials.
- Right to apply for federal employment requiring U.S. citizenship.
- Right to run for elected office.
- Freedom to pursue "life, liberty, and the pursuit of happiness."

(U. S. Citizenship and Immigration Services Citizenship Rights and Responsibilities. (2020, July 5))

The unalienable right of freedom to pursue "life, liberty, and the pursuit of happiness" is found in the Declaration of Independence. This unalienable right is a statement of principle but not the law. The legal rights are in the Bill of Rights of the U.S. Constitution.

WHAT ARE CIVIC DUTIES?

Civic duties are different from civil rights, as explained above. We use the term *duty*—or better stated, "civic duty"— to describe the responsibilities of individuals to their society at large. The United States assumes that individuals have specific responsibilities that go beyond a person's personal preference.

Below, you will find several of the responsibilities that all citizens should exercise and respect. Some of these responsibilities are legally required of every citizen, but all are important to ensure that United States of America remains a free and prosperous nation.

- Support and defend the Constitution.
- Stay informed of issues affecting your community.
- Participate in the democratic process.
- Respect and obey federal, state, and local laws.
- Respect the rights, beliefs, and opinions of others.
- Participate in your local community.
- Pay taxes honestly and on time to federal, state, and local authorities.
- Serve on a jury when called upon.
- Defend the country if the need should arise.

(U. S. Citizenship and Immigration Services Citizenship Rights and Responsibilities. (2020, July 5))

CHAPTER 4

Competing Political and Economic Philosophies

Keywords: Capitalism, Communism, Conservatives, Fascism, Liberals, Socialism.

ECONOMIC SYSTEMS AND POLITICAL PHILOSOPHIES

Traditionally, there are four major political and economic theories: capitalism, fascism, socialism, and communism. No nation has a pure form of any of these systems. Instead, countries have some form of these concepts, with the distinction being in the quantity and quality mixture each nation employs. Below is a pure definition of each theory and a short critique.

WHAT IS CAPITALISM?

Capitalism is based on the idea that human beings are motivated by needs and that progress comes about through competition. Capitalism embraces the concept of private property and that profit motivates business, trade, and even life. In the United States, capitalism is the dominant system. Please note, however, that our progressive tax system is an *anti*-capitalist structure. It argues that the more one earns, the more one pays. This system is very different from that of some capitalist countries, such as Chile, that use a "flat tax" system. The U.S. social security system and Medicare are two examples of non-capitalism. Hundreds of countries practice some form of capitalism in the world today.

WHAT IS FASCISM?

It operates a robust central government under the authority of a dictator. It may or may not have a capitalist economic system, but strict government controls exist. We might call this "government-mandated capitalism". All individuals are subservient to the state, and violence, intimidation, and racism are used to control the population. Fascists and Communists are often bitter enemies in word and action, but both philosophies emphasize central and total control of their people. Nazi Germany and Italy in the 1930s and '40s are examples of failed Fascist states.

WHAT IS SOCIALISM?

Socialism emphasizes property and trade being in the hands of the government. It promotes high taxes that are then redistributed as equal benefits for all. Many Scandinavian nations experimented with some form of socialism. These nations had extremely high tax rates, about 60%, but at least on paper, they provided social services such as free health care and education to all of their citizens.

So far, pure socialism has only worked with limited success for small nations or communities, such as communes and kibbutzim. These were rich in natural resources and had a homogeneous population. An example of a partial socialist state is Norway, a nation of under ten million people with great petroleum wealth. On the other hand, Norway's two neighbors, Denmark and Sweden, do not have these natural resources and have reverted to some form of capitalism.

WHAT IS COMMUNISM?

Communism is a mixture of political class warfare mixed with socialist ideas. Its goal is a class revolution, leading to a society where the working class owns and operates the means of production and output. So far, no pure communist society has ever been successful in the long term. The Soviet Union, China, and Cuba have attempted to create classless societies, but all have failed.

POLITICAL AND MORAL PHILOSOPHIES

Every political candidate and everyone discussing politics seems to wrap everything in a simple package and stick it on a label. These labels are so bent and twisted that you may not recognize the candidate's label once you look at the definition. When you understand the label's description, you may come to like or dislike that label.

The opposing labels are expressed linearly, with one faction on the right and its antithesis on the left. In reality, a circle seems best to represent the practices of today's factions. Communists and Fascists both use government to control the masses. In contrast, white supremacists, right-wing conservatives, and ANTIFA, left-wing liberals, use protest and violence to try and impose their will. They are side by side in the reality circle.

WHAT DO CONSERVATIVES BELIEVE?

Conservatives respect American traditions, support Judeo-Christian values, also known as traditional American values, are anti-communist and socialist, and defend Western culture. Liberty within these core values is essential. They oppose high taxes and government and labor union encroachment on entrepreneurs or public employee agencies. They support a small, deregulated government, reduced government spending, and lowered national debt, and are opposed to tax increases. Economic liberalism and fair trade are fundamental traits. The Jeffersonian maxim that the government closest to the people governs the best is an anchor for conservatives. America First is a phrase many conservatives embrace, as is Make America Great Again (MAGA).

WHAT DO LIBERALS (PROGRESSIVES) BELIEVE?

Liberalism, by definition, is a political philosophy based on liberty, consent of the governed, and equality before the law. Liberals' beliefs range from the far left to the far right. Traditionally, they supported free markets, free trade, capitalism, democracy, freedom of speech, freedom of the press, and freedom of religion. Some Modern liberals are also known as progressives. These left-leaning people embrace concepts such as environmentalism and "social justice". They are primarily secular or pseudo-secular, although some progressives morph conventional science to the level of a type of faith or religion. They focus on reducing income inequality, reforming Wall Street, eliminating private property ownership, universal health care, perceived police brutality, gender fluid acceptance, climate change, internationalism, and altering societal norms on acceptable speech. Another focus is to shift responsibility to ethnic privilege causation. Ironically, many of these people tend to be part of the very rich.

Today, many American extreme leftist liberals are activists. They reject traditional behavioral norms and definitions for individuals while requiring others to embrace their atypical behavior. They use protest, intimidation, and ostracization at educational institutions, media, and government to adopt and advance liberal ideology. Liberals use the slogans, Save our Democracy, Defund the Police, and Save the Earth.

WHAT DO THE LIBERTARIANS BELIEVE?

The Libertarians support political freedom, emphasizing freedom of choice, freedom to associate with whom you want, and individual judgment. They are skeptical of authority and state power. They range from the far left to the far right depending on their beliefs in utilizing these principles:

- The Libertarian conservative wing strongly supports capitalist private property rights. Like most forms of libertarianism, it supports civil liberties and a significant reversal of the modern welfare state.
- The Libertarian left wing wants to abolish capitalism and private ownership of the production of goods in favor of common or cooperative ownership and management. They view personal property as a barrier to freedom and liberty. These views are closely related to socialism and communism.

Several other non-mainstream groups do not fit these philosophical or political groups well. Their stated focus is on violently fighting far right or far left groups, such as white supremacists and ANTIFA, rather than through electoral means. These movements comprise separate militant groups and individuals in the United States. They engage in online activism, property damage, physical violence, and harassment against those whom they identify as fascist or racist. They tend to be anti-capitalists and include anarchists, socialists, and communists, along with some liberals and social democrats.

CHAPTER 5

The Ins-and-Outs of American Democracy

Keywords: Democracy, Electoral college, Federal republic.

WHAT IS A DEMOCRACY?

Democracy is a form of government in which citizens choose their government's policies or elect all or some of their leaders to represent their wishes. The term comes from the Greek word *demos*, meaning people, and *Kratos*, meaning power. In the United States, we understand the term to mean that we strive to provide freedom and equality for all citizens, and we have rules to ensure that all legally qualified people have an equal vote, regardless of their wealth or family background.

In a democracy and within the confines of the law, the majority decides the direction and action of their community or country.

We can divide democracy into two groups and several sub-groups. A direct democracy is where every citizen is directly involved in decision-making. Direct democracies are impractical for almost all nations as it would be impossible for all citizens to vote on every issue.

Most democratic countries solve this problem by implementing a second type of democracy called a representative democracy. We can divide representative democracies into several sub-groups. A representative democracy means that qualified citizens vote for someone to represent them. The elected representatives must look after their constituents' best interests. In an ideal world, these representatives will immerse themselves in the pros and cons of issues and then vote for what they believe will produce the best outcome for the majority of the people who elected them.

If their constituents believe their representative is ineffective or acting contrary to their wishes, they can vote them out of office during the next election. In many locales, citizens also have the right to a recall vote, that is, to remove the representative from office before the next election.

In some centralized democracies, the government gets its power and authority from the people, but few or even no autonomous government entities exist within individual divisions of the country. All government power and control occurs through the central government.

A federal republic is a federation, or a united group of states or provinces, governed by elected representatives and an elected leader. In the United States, in these subdivisions, states oversee education and infrastructure, and the federal government handles defense and monetary policies.

WHAT IS THE UNITED STATES: A DEMOCRACY, A FEDERAL REPUBLIC, OR A CONSTITUTIONAL REPUBLIC?

As noted in the previous questions, direct democracy is unworkable except in small villages. Due to the United States' history and large size, we are a type of representative democracy, defined as a federal republic.

The United States is economically, demographically, ethnically, and politically diverse. The areas and groups have unique economic strengths, weaknesses, thoughts, and needs. A central government cannot make every law benefit all the nation's citizens. As a remedy, our founders provided layers of government. They assumed that governments closest to their citizens—that is, local governments—best understand the needs of their citizens. State governments facilitate cooperation and interactions between local governments. The central government, the United States federal government, oversees the interaction between states and represents the entire nation to foreign governments.

The United States is a type of federal republic, a constitutional republic, where each state within the United States has power and authority granted by the U.S. Constitution that the central government cannot modify. The state's authority and power cover areas different from the control and management of the central government.

The United States Constitution has been an excellent framework for a successful society; here are some of the reasons why it works well:

- Most Americans have a sense of fundamental fairness.
- Most Americans respect the U.S. Constitution even when decisions do not work to their particular benefit.
- There is a general set of ethical principles that most people support as a moral compass, a general sense of right and wrong. Our structure is one of the most successful and, to a greater or lesser degree, the most followed form of government in the history of the world.
- Most Americans respect the fact that the Constitution is the ultimate political authority.

WHY DO WE HAVE STATES INSTEAD OF OTHER GOVERNMENTAL ENTITIES?

The history of European settlements in North America has significantly impacted the formation of a government structure that has made us one of the most prosperous countries in history. If you look at our beginnings, European countries came to North America and established settlements that grew into colonies. The Dutch, English, French, and Spanish all established settlements.

The colonies adopted the thoughts and ideas of their parent countries. The European countries fought and traded colonies for about one hundred and fifty years. Eventually, Great Britain acquired the thirteen colonies that became the birthplace of the United States. During the War for Independence from Great Britain, the colonies acted together against their common enemy. After the war, each former colony wanted to operate independently. Based on the French concept of "état" *versus* "province", they translated the term état as "state" to mean an "independent" entity rather than a subdivision set up by a national government. This term reflects that the states formed the federal government rather than the federal government creating subsections called provinces.

These states formed a loose union through the Articles of Confederation that allowed little authority and power to the central governing body, leaving most of the power with the individual states. Unsurprisingly, this system did not work, and one big problem was that the confederation could not protect the country from common enemies. For this reason, they wrote a new law of the land, the Constitution, and all thirteen states eventually adopted it.

The Constitution provided for a national representative democracy and a federal republic. The founders and citizens were smart enough to realize that states had diverse needs and opinions, so they left much of the power and decisions to the individual states. The United States has a multiple governmental system, with cities, towns, and counties having local governments, the states having governments that represent the interests of all their citizens, and a workable federal government.

The Constitution provided a foundation so that all these various levels of government could serve the unique needs of their populations and still work together in areas that provide the most benefit to the future citizens of the United States. When new states were added to the original thirteen, each of these new states and their citizens received the same benefits as the states before them.

It bears repeating: This model of government is one of the reasons the U.S. is one of the most successful countries in the history of the world.

Within the U.S.A., there are fifty states, and each of them has these common characteristics:

- Statehood is permanent, not temporary. The Civil War settled the issue of states having the right to leave the United States.
- States have a specific territory with recognized boundaries.
- States have a functioning political and administrative organization, known as a state government, that must serve the interests of those living there.
- States are responsible for many economic activities.
- Each state has the authority to make and enforce laws if these laws do not conflict with the principles of the U.S. Constitution.
- Each state has the power of taxation.
- Each state has the power to have a militia, often called the National Guard.
- States have those powers that are not explicitly given to the federal government.

WHAT IS THE ELECTORAL COLLEGE, AND HOW DOES IT DIFFER FROM THE POPULAR VOTE?

Our election system encompasses the highly beneficial attributes of U.S. diversity through the Electoral College. Diversity was a miraculous essential part of the founding of the United States, and it still is today!

The Dutch, English, French, and Spanish all significantly impacted the type of government that has made us one of history's most successful countries. Their colonies adopted the thoughts and ideas of their parent countries from across the Atlantic Ocean. Fighting and trading of colonial land in the New World occurred for about one hundred and fifty years. Finally, Great Britain took control of the thirteen colonies of what was to become the original United States of America. When the War for Independence from Great Britain occurred, the colonies acted together against their common enemy. But that unity dissolved after their victory. Each former colony had diverse needs and priorities.

Soon after the War of Independence from Great Britain, the former colonies created the Articles of Confederation. The states retained the majority of power in the Articles, and the central government was granted little authority. This form of government failed, and change was needed. Representatives from each of the states wrote a constitution that was eventually adopted by all the thirteen states.

This Constitution provided for a federal republic. The goal was to create a balance between the new nation's diverse parts and to allow representation to serve the needs of each demographic and cultural region within the United States. The Constitution affirms the benefit of diverse groups acting independently and in unity by creating various levels of government and also through the Electoral College. The constitutional structure serves and represents the unique contributions and needs of each governmental body's population. The Constitution also provides the foundation for all these levels of government to work together to provide the most benefit to the greatest number of American citizens.

Today, we are more diverse than ever! We have added states that are far different than the original thirteen states. We have different ethnic and religious backgrounds, and this diversity is widely and often celebrated today in America. A recent poll said ninety percent of Americans are satisfied with their life (McCarthy, 2020).

But there is more to diversity than this. Every day, 330 million Americans use energy to heat their homes, cook their food, and get to work. Most of us live in buildings or houses. We use computer software to run our businesses, pay our bills, and monitor our health. We all eat food and drink water daily.

A huge part of our banking occurs in New York, Chicago, and San Francisco. These areas of the country produce little solar or petroleum energy or grow very little of the food that feeds our nation. North Dakota, Oklahoma, and Texas produce a substantial amount of the energy used in the U.S., but compared to the large urban centers on the East and West Coast, they have fewer urban jobs. California gets a sizable portion of water from the Colorado River, mainly from snow melting in Colorado.

"Rural areas cover 97 percent of the nation's land area but contain 19.3 percent of the population (about 60 million people)", Census Bureau Director John H. Thompson said. (American Community Survey: 2011–2015, 2016).

These rural areas produce most of our energy, food, and water.

Because of this diversity and being able to work together, we are the world's most important economy.

Our Constitution is a keystone of our success. It gives the states that provide essentials like energy and food but have a minority of the population a voice in the election of the President and the U. S. Senate. That voice is through the Electoral College.

The Electoral College consists of 538 electors. A state has one elector for each member of the House of Representatives plus two electors for each state's Senators. The District of Columbia has three electors and is regarded as a state under the 23rd Amendment of the Constitution in the Electoral College.

A majority of 270 electoral votes is needed to elect the President.

When you vote for a Presidential candidate, you are voting for your candidate's preferred electors. Each candidate running for President in your state has their own group of electors.

Each state's electoral votes are counted in a joint session of Congress on the 6th of January in the year following the meeting of the electors. Members of the House and Senate conduct the official count of electoral votes. The winners of the Electoral College vote are declared the next President and Vice President of the United States (National Archives, 2023).

CHAPTER 6

The Founding Documents of American Democracy

Keywords: Articles of confederation, Declaration of independence, President, President's cabinet, United states constitution.

WHAT IS THE DECLARATION OF INDEPENDENCE?

The Declaration of Independence set the moral justification for our revolt against British tyranny. Americans wanted all the rights of Englishmen, but England held that the colonists were there to benefit the Crown and Parliament. "No taxation without representation!" was a familiar cry. The Declaration of Independence stands as a beacon of light, expressing the best of American ideals.

WHAT ARE THE ARTICLES OF CONFEDERATION?

After winning independence from England in 1783, the United States tried to govern itself using the "Articles of Confederation". This document gave the states the majority of the power. The Articles of Confederation proved to be unworkable. For this reason, the founding fathers decided to write a formal national constitution that gave the federal government much greater power.

WHAT IS THE U.S. CONSTITUTION?

The preamble, or introduction, to the U.S. Constitution needs no introduction. It tells us why the Constitution was written and describes the values our country seeks to uphold. The preamble reads as follows:

"WE, the PEOPLE of the UNITED STATES, in order to form a more perfect union, establish justice, ensure domestic tranquility, provide for the common defense, promote the general welfare, and secure the blessings of liberty to ourselves and our posterity, do ordain and establish this Constitution for the United States of America" (We, the people of the United States, in order to form a more perfect union..., n.d.).

The U.S. Constitution might be compared to the rules of a game. It is the basis for all laws in the United States, and any law that goes against the principles expressed in the Constitution ceases to be legitimate.

"The members of the Constitutional Convention signed the United States Constitution on September 17, 1787, in Philadelphia, Pennsylvania. The Constitutional Convention convened in response to dissatisfaction with the Articles of Confederation and the need for a strong centralized government. After four months of secret debate and many compromises, the proposed Constitution was submitted to the states for approval. Although the vote was close in some states, the Constitution was eventually ratified, and the new Federal government came into existence in 1789. The Constitution established the U.S. government as it exists today" (Ken Drexler, 2019).

Fashion trends come and go. We have had tight blue jeans, baggie jeans, and tight jeans again. Amazingly, some people believe the Constitution's importance is like fashions in clothing, ever-evolving. Some of these people believe the Constitution is useless or outdated and, therefore, want to change those parts that do not fit their desires. Many others will argue that our Constitution is the backbone of the laws and values that have made the U.S. a great country. The latter believe that to throw parts of it away for "political fashion" would destroy the nation and its people.

TO WHOM DID THE CONSTITUTION ASSIGN POWER?

The Constitution formed a three-part system of government in which no one branch was to have more power than the other two branches. This three-part system of government is based on what is called separation of powers. The three constitutionally mandated centers of power are:

1. The Legislative Branch comprises the House of Representatives and the Senate. This branch is responsible for making laws.
2. The Executive Branch, headed by the President, is tasked with enforcing the laws and setting foreign policy.
3. The Judicial Branch settles disputes using the United States Constitution as its secular "Bible".

WHY DO WE HAVE A VICE PRESIDENT?

As noted, the President is the head of the executive branch. The founding fathers also realized that all presidents are mortal and can die during their term of office or, for some other reason, cannot assume the duties of their office. In that case, the Vice President takes over from the President. The vice president's official duties are:

- To preside over the Senate and to break a tie vote
- To assume the presidency if the President is incapable of carrying out their responsibilities
- To perform other duties as assigned by the President

WHAT IS CONGRESS?

The word congress has two common meanings. The official meaning of Congress refers to both the Senate (upper House composed of two senators from each state and elected for a six-year term) and the lower House (House of Representatives consisting of 435 members who are elected for two-year terms of office and proportioned according to the population ranking of each state). In common parlance, however, the House of Representatives is often called "Congress" or simply "the House". Context is needed to clarify the terms.

HOW DOES AN IDEA BECOME THE LAW?

The path from an idea to a law of the land is long and treacherous, and most ideas never become a law. The American system is designed to be slow and deliberate to eliminate quick or emotional changes to our government that could result in unforeseen consequences, unfairly punish people or groups, or enact unconstitutional laws.

A law starts with individuals or groups submitting their ideas to someone in Congress or their staff. The groups are permitted to engage lobbyists who are professionals and who know how to increase the chances of turning an idea into a law.

Conceivably, promising ideas will be championed by that member of Congress, who will recruit other congressional members to write the proposed Bill legally and sponsor it before the appropriate committee in the House of Representatives or the appropriate committee in the Senate. All bills that raise revenue must start in the House of Representatives.

The committee will consider the submitted Bill and may suggest changes, and if they vote in favor of the Bill, it will be passed to the committee's total body, House or Senate, for consideration. If this body passes the Bill, it goes to the other chamber and slogs through the same process.

If both houses of Congress pass the Bill, it will be sent to a joint committee of both houses to work out a compromise between the version the House passed and the Senate version.

If they agree on a compromise bill, it will go before both congressional bodies for a vote.

If Congress passes it, the Bill is sent to the President of the United States to consider signing it into law.

WHAT IS A PRESIDENTIAL VETO?

For a piece of legislation to become law, the President must sign it. If the President signs the legislation, the process has finished, and the Bill becomes law. The President also has the power not to sign a piece of legislation, and this refusal to sign is called a "veto". If the President vetoes the legislation, then it returns to Congress. Once returned to Congress, the House of Representatives and the Senate can try to override the veto. If two-thirds of each House (House of Representatives and Senate) votes to override the President's veto, it becomes law. If they fail to override the veto, the Bill dies and does not become a law.

During the end of a congressional session, there is also a provision where the President can leave the Bill unsigned, and the Bill dies.

This outlined process is simplified compared to all the maneuvers and procedures of our government. It is exceedingly rare for an idea to become a law and change our governance.

WHAT IS THE PRESIDENT'S CABINET, AND WHAT ARE THEIR FUNCTIONS?

The President's cabinet is created by Article 2 Section 2 of U.S. constitution, that states, "he may require the opinion in writing of the principal officer in each of the executive departments upon any subject relating to the duties of their respective offices---" (We, the people of the United States, in order to form a more perfect union..., n.d.).

The fifteen members advise the President, carry out the duties of the Executive Branch, and are in the line of succession if there is a vacancy in the Presidency of the United States. The order of succession is Vice President, Speaker of the House, and Senate President pro tempore, and then the succession goes down the line of cabinet members in the order the offices were created. The appropriate Senate committee reviews them, and then they must be confirmed to office by the whole Senate.

This Cabinet office is listed in the succession order:

Department of State

Direct the foreign service and immigration policy and administer the Department of State.

Department of the Treasury

Responsible for creating and recommending domestic and international financial, economic, and tax policy.

Department of Defense (DOD)

All matters related to the Department of Defense.

Department of Justice (Attorney General)

Head of the DOJ and chief law enforcement officer, including the Federal Bureau of Investigation and the U.S. Marshals Service.

Department of the Interior (DOI)

Management and conservation of federal land and natural resources, and head of the Bureau of Land Management, the United States Geological Survey, the Bureau of Indian Affairs, and the National Park Service.

Department of Agriculture (USDA)

Head of United States Forest Service, United States Food Safety and Inspection Service, and The Food Stamp Program.

Department of Commerce

Responsible for fostering, promoting, and developing foreign and domestic commerce for American businesses and industries.

Department of Labor

Head of the United States Department of Labor, which enforces and suggests laws involving unions, the workplace, and issues involving business-person controversies.

Department of Health and Human Services (HHS)

They advise the President on health, welfare, and income security programs.

Department of Housing and Urban Development (HUD)

To increase homeownership, support community development, and increase access to affordable housing without discrimination.

Department of Transportation (DOT)

Head of the Federal Aviation Administration, the Federal Highway Administration, the Federal Railroad Administration, and the National Highway Traffic Safety Administration.

Department of Energy (DOE)

They are focused on energy production and regulation, developing more efficient energy sources, energy education, radioactive waste disposal, and maintenance of environmental quality.

Department of Education

Directs policies, programs, and activities related to education.

Department of Veteran Affairs

The department oversees veterans' benefits, health care, and national veterans' memorials and cemeteries.

Department of Homeland Security (DHS)

Includes the Coast Guard, the Federal Protective Service, U.S. Customs and Border Protection (which consists of the United States Border Patrol), U.S. Immigration and Customs Enforcement, the United States Secret Service, and the Federal Emergency Management Agency.

WHAT IS AN EXECUTIVE ORDER?

An executive order is a signed, written, and published mandate from the President that directs the federal government's operations. Congress cannot pass legislation to overturn it, but it can enact legislation to remove funding, making it ineffective. A sitting president can overturn an executive order by issuing another executive order.

Courts can strike down executive orders by declaring them unconstitutional.

All but one President has issued at least one executive order. George Washington was the first; Franklin Roosevelt issued the most, over 3,700.

WHAT IS THE FUNCTION OF THE JUDICIAL BRANCH?

The Constitution establishes the judicial branch of the federal government, declaring,

"The judicial power of the United States shall be vested in one supreme Court, and in such inferior Courts as the Congress may from time to time ordain and establish". (We, the people of the United States, in order to form a more perfect union..., n.d.)

The court system settles disputes using the United States Constitution as its secular "Bible".

There are three levels of the federal judiciary: 94 district courts, 13 courts of appeals, and the United States Supreme Court.

State judiciaries are also established to rule on state laws.

The district courts conduct trials for disputes involving federal laws or crimes with a judge, a lifetime position appointed by the U.S. President and confirmed by the Senate. They try the actual dispute or controversy and may or may not reach decisions with the assistance of a jury.

The courts of appeals jurisdictions have a number of judges that oversee the district courts in their jurisdictions. A dispute where the district court decision is appealed is referred to a panel of three judges. This panel of judges considers if the decision by the district court is in accordance with the U.S. Constitution. The judges will issue an opinion which will bind the district courts.

The U.S. Supreme Court comprises one Chief Justice and eight Associate Justices, nominated by the President, confirmed by the Senate, and have life tenure.

This Court has the first authority over disputes between states.

The Supreme Court can hear appeals to the Supreme Court from the courts of appeal if four of the judges agree to listen to the case. The lower court ruling stands if the Supreme Court refuses to hear the case.

This Court agrees to hear about one percent of the appeals submitted to it.

When they hear a case, interested parties submit briefs or arguments that support their side; they then make oral arguments to the judges, and the judges meet in private to discuss the case's merits and then issue a written opinion.

The decisions of the Supreme Court are final and binding.

WHAT IS THE BILL OF RIGHTS?

When the Constitution was approved, many founding fathers felt there should be limits on the federal government's power. Two years after the Constitution was ratified, the first ten amendments to the U.S. Constitution were adopted (1791). These ten amendments (or additions) are the Bill of Rights. Although technically, there is no such thing as the popularly known "Bill of Rights". This common phrase refers to the first ten amendments to the U.S. Constitution and guarantees many of our fundamental freedoms; hence, the public often calls these amendments fondly by the term "the Bill of Rights".

These are the freedoms guaranteed under the Bill of Rights:

Amendment 1: Freedom of speech, religion, and the press.

Amendment 2: The right to bear arms.

Amendment 3: The right not to be forced to quarter soldiers.

Amendment 4: The right to be free of unreasonable searches and seizures.

Amendment 5: Freedom from self-incrimination, the right to due process of law, and freedom from double jeopardy.

Amendment 6: The right to a speedy and public trial.

Amendment 7: In civil cases, the right to trial by jury.

Amendment 8: Freedom from excessive bail and cruel and unusual punishment.

Amendment 9: The right of the courts to abridge illegal actions done by the legislature or the executive.

Amendment 10: Powers not stated in the Constitution are to be reserved to the states.

WHAT IS BUREAUCRACY, AND IS IT ELECTED?

Politicians often have limited terms of office. Thus, governments develop a professional class of people who specialize in particular parts of the government. For example, the Department of State has bureaucrats who are specialists in foreign affairs, the Defense Department has specialists in military matters, and the Department of Energy oversees oil, gas, electricity, *etc*. These departments receive their budget from the Congress and are part of the national budget. Nevertheless, there can be philosophical differences, which create tensions between the civil servants, many of whom have lifetime appointments, and the elected officials. Although their budgets depend on Congress, in reality, many of these appointees have lifetime positions, and there is little congressional oversight of many people in the bureaucracy.

Our federal government is a vast, multilayered bureaucracy. In addition, there are state, county, city, and many other government entities. Their focus is to serve the people of the United States.

Therefore, some argue that we have an unofficial fourth branch of government, the permanent bureaucracy. The question of how much power permanent bureaucracies should have is highly debated.

We decide in our elections how much and where we believe the U.S. government should be involved in our lives. Our elected representatives pass or repeal the laws that define how the government will affect us. They legislate how much of our money we will pay in taxes.

The government stays involved in our lives through bureaucrats. They are not elected but appointed or hired to do the work of the government. Federal government agencies look at the laws and decide how they should be applied and how to administrate them. Government employees are there to benefit or help us send our money to the government. In 2023, it is estimated that ununiformed employees who work for the Federal Government total about 4.33 million (Federal Workforce Statistics Sources: OPM and OMB 2022).

WHAT IS THE "DEEP STATE"?

Many government and private industry workers have strong opinions about the importance of the impact of their jobs. In some federal elections, the citizens elect representatives who want to change the direction of the nation or a state's direction. For many people, change is hard, especially when the public, through its elected officials, decides to change course. People who have held the same position for multiple years often believe they know what is best. At times, these entrenched managers actively reject innovative ideas or directions. Often, these unelected bureaucrats who may even ignore or refuse to act on the will of the people are called "the deep state".

Resistance to change has led many people to believe a "deep state" exists within governments. According to the theory, governments including workers who see elected officials as merely transitory figureheads. These officials do not accept the people's representatives' right to make changes and often resist those who might have different ideas from their own. Those who accept the deep state notion believe it might extend to multiple agencies and layers within a government's bureaucracy. The deep state prevents change or policy implementation in several ways, including what is known as "slow walking" a policy or even outright refusal to implement a policy.

WHAT ARE THE TERMS POTUS, FLOTUS, AND SCOTUS?

The earliest recorded use of any of these terms is from 1879 when SCOTUS (Supreme Court of the United States) appeared in a book titled *The Phillips Telegraphic Code for the Rapid Transmission by Telegraph*. This work, written by Walter P. Phillips, was one of many code books that allowed people to send inexpensive or secret messages *via* the telegraph. Telegraphs were priced based on length, so one wanted to use as few words as possible.

The next acronym is POTUS, short for "President of the United States", used as early as 1895. POTUS also began as an abbreviation used by telegraphic code operators.

Although SCOTUS and POTUS are the most familiar words, they are far from the only ones. FLOTUS, First Lady of the United States, appeared in the 1980s, where it may have originated as the Secret Service's code name for Nancy Reagan (Merriam-Webster, 2023).

CHAPTER 7

The Media and U.S. Elections

Keywords: Fake news, Feelings, Media, News outlet, Opinions, PBS/Public Broadcasting Service.

WHAT IS THE ROLE OF THE MEDIA?

The media exists in many different forms. In the modern world, print and radio are the oldest modes, followed by cinema, television, and now the Internet and social media. We can easily divide the media into news reporting, opinion, and entertainment. Most Americans recognize that most media outlets slant their work, despite claiming to be unbiased, and rarely are objective in their reporting.

We rely on the media to:

• Inform and educate.
• Investigate and inform us of questionable activities.
• Be a platform for opinions.
• Be a platform to publicize activities and ideas.
• Entertain.

ARE THE MEDIA PROTECTED UNDER THE FIRST AMENDMENT?

The answer to this question depends on how one defines "media". The U.S. Constitution protects a free press (see Amendment 1), and most legal scholars have expanded this right to include the electronic press. At this time, some argue that this expansion might be an overreach. Two arguments against applying this protection to the media are as follows.

The media may be as much entertainment as informative.

A few oligarchs control social media platforms by giving themselves the right to censorship. They see themselves as more intelligent than the average person. For this reason, they have declared it their right to decide what may or may not be presented or read.

Most legal scholars argue that it is necessary to err on the side of free expression. Nevertheless, individuals hurt by the media are now suing media giants and often winning large settlements. How these lawsuits impact the media and its accuracy or lack of truthfulness is unfolding political reality.

WHAT ARE THE NEWS OUTLETS IN THE UNITED STATES?

In the United States, the three classical networks, ABC, CBS, and NBC, host various news and entertainment programs on television and internet programming.

CNN, FOX News, and MSNBC are major news and political opinion networks on television and the Internet. Other notable outlets in this genre are Newsmax and OAN.

There is also publicly funded PBS, which is "supposedly" unbiased on television and the Internet.

A multitude of syndicated radio and internet talk show programs are broadcast.

The Associated Press, the New York Times, the Wall Street Journal, the Washington Post, and USA Today are major print media outlets. Most communities have some form of a printed and or online press. Many of these local papers receive their news from the primary media sources listed above.

Increasingly, many people rely on social media and the Internet. The Internet allows U.S. citizens to access news from around the world and in the language of their choice.

DO NEWS OUTLETS HAVE POLITICAL LEANINGS?

Yes. A small number of people or organizations in the history of the world have remained unbiased when offered the chance to gain power and wealth from supporting an individual or organization. A well-used truism from the 1976 movie *All the President's Men* is "Follow the money". Unbiased, objective reporting of the news based on facts, not opinion, or giving fair treatment to both sides of an issue is considered neutral reporting. Most news outlets claim to be neutral, but they are not. The vast majority of news media tends to be center to center-left. U.S. media outlets are not required to state their political biases.

WHAT ARE THE POLITICAL LEANINGS OF EACH MAJOR U.S. NEWS OUTLET?

Left-leaning means more slanted toward Progressivism, and right-leaning means slanted more toward Conservatism.

ABC	Left
NBC	Left to very left
CBS	Left
Newsmax	Right
NPR	Very left
OAN	Right
Fox	Right to center
New York Times	Very left
USA Today	Left
Washington Post	Very left
Washington Times	Right

WHAT IS A FACT-CHECKER?

Hypothetically, a fact checker is a neutral person who seeks to ensure that politicians state the facts correctly—and speak the truth—during speeches, press conferences, and political debates. The same responsibility applies to print and Internet postings.

HOW DOES ONE BECOME A FACT-CHECKER?

These people often work for a media outlet. There are questions about the accuracy of fact-checkers, and there are now fact-checkers checking the fact-checkers.

ARE ALL FACT-CHECKERS UNBIASED?

No. If the media outlet is biased, the same will hold true for the fact-checker it employs. Most entities will not have employees who disagree with the organization's talking points.

WHAT IS FAKE NEWS? HOW DOES FAKE NEWS DIFFER FROM MISINFORMATION AND OUTRIGHT FABRICATION?

Fake news has little or no basis and is created to achieve a political goal. Stories that stated the COVID-19 vaccination will keep you from getting COVID-19 were incorrect or fake news. Misinformation is the unintentional reporting of false facts. When the misinformation is presented as correct, and the informer knows the contrary to be the case, gaslighting as fabrication.

HOW DO I KNOW REAL NEWS FROM FAKE NEWS?

Check the story from all sides of an issue and compare the news item with other media from home and abroad, both liberal and conservative. Ask yourself if the information has facts to support the statements. Take a mental step back, clear your mind of your opinions, and evaluate.

HOW DO I DIFFERENTIATE FACTS FROM "FEELINGS" AND "OPINIONS"?

If the person says, "I believe that" or "I feel that," you are listening to a feeling. Listen for the "that" conjunction. If used, you have a feeling rather than a fact.

HOW IMPORTANT IS SOCIAL MEDIA?

Extremely important! Social media has a major impact on modern elections. It might be almost impossible to win an election without some exposure on social media.

The effect on all of us cannot be underestimated! Almost everyone in the United States is now connected to the Internet. It is nearly impossible to search the Internet for a person, place, thing, subject, or opinion and not find some information.

IS EVERYTHING ON SOCIAL MEDIA TRUTHFUL AND CORRECT?

Of course not! People will strongly disagree and waste considerable time arguing over something as unimportant as the color of a dress shown on the Internet. Consider how much time and effort these people and others will spend convincing you to support their beliefs. You must ferret out accurate information from misinformation, facts from urban legends, and truth from published lies to confuse or mislead.

DO POLITICIANS AND PEOPLE WITH A POLITICAL AGENDA USE SOCIAL MEDIA OR THE INTERNET TO THEIR ADVANTAGE?

The easy, and unfortunately obvious, answer is yes! In 2019, Congress investigated the effect of social media on elections. They questioned Dr. Robert Epstein, former editor-in-chief of *Psychology Today*, who was a self-proclaimed "solid public supporter of Hillary Clinton". His research, he stated, indicated that in the 2016 election, **Google added about 2.6 million votes to** then-presidential candidate **Hillary Clinton**. Alphabet, Inc., Google's parent company, was Hillary's number-one financial donor in 2016.

WHAT WOULD BE THE IMPACT IF ALL THE SOCIAL MEDIA GIANTS SUPPORTED ONE CANDIDATE? HOW MANY VOTES WOULD BE IN PLAY?

The answer is shocking. The effect of social media giants' biased action would not cost the company a dime and would be "without people's knowledge and without leaving a paper trail."

Do not believe everything you see or read on the Internet. An included link to C-Span is given below to educate yourself on the facts revealed in Dr. Robert Epstein's testimony.

https://www.c-span.org/video/?c4814811/user-clip-ted-cruz-questions-robert-epstein-big-tech-election-interference (C-SPAN, 2019).

HOW CAN I HELP A CANDIDATE OR SUPPORT MY POSITION ON AN ISSUE THROUGH SOCIAL MEDIA?

There are multiple ways to help on social media. These include:

• Monitor social media and react when you read an untruth or something outlandish. Caution: do not always react, but only when the subject is important, and you have facts to support your rebuttal.
• Send out articles to your social media colleagues. Hopefully, your contacts appreciate facts and logic instead of twisted or half-truths, things taken out of context, or lies.

The old saying, "You can catch more flies with honey than vinegar", is true. There are times we all say things that hurt someone we care about. If a good friend posts something hurtful, connect with them privately and positively explain your thoughts.

Most of the time, people will appreciate your honesty and learn from your input. There are people, nevertheless, who copy and paste truly outrageous things. It is obvious they do not ever consider both sides of an issue, and nothing will get them to realize that the intellectual garbage they post is untrue. Try to reply with facts, but you usually are just wasting your time trying to show a biased person the light.

Responsibly use social media. Do not use hurtful words, avoid insulting a person due to their gender, national origin, religious preference, or race, and always be truthful!

CHAPTER 8

The American Political Party System

Keywords: Candidate, Democrats, Identity Politics, Political parties, Republicans.

WHAT ARE POLITICAL PARTIES?

Political parties are individuals who band together around a common idea or candidate. Some countries have one ruling party; typically, they are countries with an authoritarian government. In contrast, some countries with parliamentary-based governments have a multitude of parties.

HOW MANY PARTIES DO WE HAVE IN THE U.S.?

Currently, the United States has two major political parties and several smaller parties. Both major parties have sub-sections called "wings". Primary elections usually determine control of the two major parties. There is no limit to the number of parties that can run in elections, although many states have specific requirements to be able to appear on an election ballot.

WHAT IS THE HISTORY OF THE TWO MAJOR PARTIES, AND WHAT ARE THEIR FUNDAMENTAL BELIEFS?

The Democratic Party, formed in the 1830s, dominated the southern states, opposed the expansion of federal power, and was considered the ordinary person's party.

Formed in 1854, Republicans, during the 1860s, dominated the northern states, supporting a strong central government over states' rights, and passed laws that made African Americans equal under the law.

In 1936, the Democratic Party switched philosophies. Democrat Franklin Roosevelt won reelection with his New Deal and created welfare, pension, and work programs in an attempt to end the Great Depression.

In 1965, a move toward a stronger federal government was enhanced by Lyndon Johnson's Great Society programs, significantly increasing the power in Washington, D.C. At that time, the southern states gradually changed to the GOP (the Republican Party) because the Republicans took up the philosophy of limited government. Basically, the parties have switched sides. Before the twenty-first century, there was the common belief that the Democrats represented the interests of the less well-to-do and minorities. In the twenty-first century, the parties switched, with the Republicans representing the less affluent and the Democrats becoming the party of the rich.

HOW IMPORTANT IS A U.S. PARTY PLATFORM?

Party platforms give a general idea as to the direction of a particular party. They are meant to be broad general statements. There are no consequences in the United States for not implementing a position stated in a party platform, and candidates, once elected, legally are not required to follow the platform's dictates.

HOW DOES ONE JOIN A POLITICAL PARTY?

Joining a political party depends on state laws. In many states, one declares a political affiliation upon registering to vote. In other states, choosing to vote in a party's primary election automatically makes one a member of that party. Check with your county clerk about how one joins a political party in your state. Many people choose not to join a political party and are called "independents".

DO I HAVE TO SUPPORT A POLITICAL PARTY TO WHICH I HAVE JOINED?

You can join a political party by donating to it, registering to be a member, or calling the party headquarters. If you are a legal voter, the party will gladly enroll you. Voting in a primary election obligates you to do nothing except when there is a runoff election after a primary election. You cannot vote for party A in the main primary election and then vote in party B's runoff election.

WHAT ARE THE ADVANTAGES AND DISADVANTAGES OF BELONGING TO A PARTICULAR PARTY?

If you want to be involved in candidate selection or policy, actively being involved in a particular party makes sense. Being a member of a party can be both expensive and time-consuming, so it is a matter of how active you want to be and how much money and time you wish to commit.

HOW DO I LEARN ABOUT WHAT A POLITICAL PARTY SUPPORTS?

Political parties publish platforms at their national conventions. It is important to understand that no U.S. politician must follow their party platform. These are philosophical positions that can easily change. It is a good idea to research individual candidates. In most elections, the candidate's headquarters will be more than happy to answer questions on specific topics.

CAN I CHANGE MY POLITICAL REGISTRATION?

Yes. In most states, this involves merely telling someone during a primary election that you want to vote in the other party's primary election.

WHAT QUESTIONS DO I WANT TO ASK A CANDIDATE OR LEARN FROM HIS PLATFORM?

No candidate will match 100% of a voter's opinions. The best thing to do is prioritize issues and then ask those questions that are your top priority.

WILL I FIND A CANDIDATE WHO AGREES WITH ME ON EVERY POLITICAL POSITION?

No. Most people cannot find a spouse who agrees with them on every issue! Life is a series of compromises, so pick the candidate whose position on your priorities best matches yours.

HOW DO I KNOW THE CANDIDATE HAS THE COUNTRY'S BEST INTEREST AT HEART?

The answer to this question is that until the person is elected and puts forth their proposals, we are merely making an educated or emotional decision rather than being certain. Although no one can tell the future, a few guidelines can help predict what a candidate might do once s/he takes the oath of office.

One effective evaluation method is to "Follow the Money". Who might economically benefit from this proposal? Who supports it, and who would become financially more affluent if the proposal were adopted? In other words, who would benefit, make money, and become more powerful if the proposal became law?

A second way is to look at similar proposals either from the past or from other democratic countries. For example, there is a current debate about whether the United States should create a universal or single-payer healthcare system. Ask yourself: What have other nations enacted? Where has a universal health care policy worked or failed? What were the reasons for the policy's failures or successes?

Still, another method is to examine the party's policies to which the candidate belongs. Do you agree with the overall policies of the candidate's party? Does the candidate agree with their party platform, and if not, why is the candidate running as a member of that party? If they disagree with their party on issues, will they have the power to stand up against their party?

Remember that sometimes politicians do what they say they will do. Would you be happy if the politician were to carry out their promises? How would these promises help or hurt the nation and you as an individual?

HOW DO I RANK ISSUES OF IMPORTANCE?

Each person will have a different ranking system. Organize and test the opinions in your mind. If you need clarification about your beliefs, research the facts about the issue. Then, decide what is most important to you, your family, and your country.

Often, economic issues take high priority. Some people will look at foreign policy issues, while others will rank domestic policy on a higher plateau. Ranking issues of importance tells you as much about yourself as it does about the candidate's position.

WHAT IS IDENTITY POLITICS?

This term often has a negative connotation. It refers to judging a person not by their ideas or abilities but by the candidate's "identity" group. This concept becomes exceedingly tricky when a person has multiple identities, such as an African-American Jewish woman opposing a gay Latino who also happens to be black. Under these circumstances, when we vote for the candidate's identity and not the candidate's position, we are reduced to judging a person by skin color, gender, or ethnic or religious grouping. That is called prejudice!

HOW DOES IDENTITY POLITICS DIFFER FROM ETHNIC/RACIAL POLITICS OR GENDER POLITICS?

In reality, there is not much difference. All groupings that lump people by physical characteristics, not their ideas or abilities, are identity politics.

DO RACIAL OR ETHNIC GROUPS VOTE ALIKE?

No, though, the media might have us think so. Most Americans believe that the basis for the United States democracy is that everyone should have the right to life, liberty, and the pursuit of happiness but not the ability to elevate a group to the detriment of another. However, it would be wrong to overlook our peers' influence on us because we share common experiences with them.

DOES THE CANDIDATE'S PERSONAL LIFE MATTER?

The answer to this question tells you a great deal about yourself. It is best to distinguish moral failings from personality dislikes. Most people tend to excuse the personal failings of a candidate whose priorities match theirs and fail to forgive the weaknesses of an opposition candidate. The bottom line is that we are not God; we all have failings. We are all human.

HOW DO I INFLUENCE A CANDIDATE OR ELECTED OFFICIAL?

There are many ways to influence a candidate or elected official. Their local offices will appear in the telephone book or on the Internet.

Here are some of the most common ways:

- Contributions. Candidates and officeholders need money and tend to listen to those who contribute to their campaigns;
- Well-written letters or cyber-communications, such as emails or Facebook posts. Always add a title to your signature and provide a way for the office to respond;

- Petitions from constituents and
- Make respectful telephone calls to the candidate or elected official's office. Tell them you will follow up, and then do it!

CHAPTER 9

Political and Economic Influences: Lobbyists and Monetary Donations

Keywords: Bundler, Down ballot, Lobbyist, Political donations.

WHAT IS A LOBBYIST?

Political lobbyists work to influence actions, government decisions, and policies. They must be registered, but they do not necessarily receive a salary. Often, they represent specific industries and "lobby" in favor or against legislation that might help or hurt the industry or cause they are supporting.

WHAT IS A BUNDLER AND A PAC, AND WHEN DOES IT BECOME DARK MONEY?

Bundler is another word for *fundraiser*. They collect contributions for a political candidate or party. PAC stands for Political Action Committee. Like fundraisers, they work for specific ideals, political policies, and legislative positions or causes. They collect money to promote a policy or stop it from happening. They are not necessarily aligned with a political party. They can and often contribute to more than one candidate or party vying for the same elected office.

ARE POLITICAL DONATIONS PUBLIC?

Political donations are public, but when money is given to influence political outcomes through politically active organizations where the donors are kept private, these donated funds are referred to as "Dark Money". These organizations can be politically active nonprofits such as 501(c)(4)s that choose not to reveal their funding sources or opaque nonprofits and shell companies where the bulk of their funding cannot be traced back to the original donor.

IS CONTRIBUTING TO A POLITICAL PARTY LEGAL, AND HOW IS IT DONE?

Yes! However, there are specific laws on how much you can donate to a particular party or candidate. To know the laws in your state, contact its board of elections. To contribute to a party, you can answer a solicitation, contact a political party or candidate, or donate to a PAC or Bundler.

WHERE SHOULD I SEND MY CHECK? DO I NEED TO HAVE A LARGE FORTUNE?

You must decide whom to support and how much you wish to donate. You can also contribute to a political party; most political candidates have a special fund with a treasurer in charge of that fund. There is no minimum donation. Every citizen has the right and privilege to donate to their chosen candidate.

SHOULD I DONATE TO A LARGE ORGANIZATION OR GO STRAIGHT TO THE CANDIDATE I SUPPORT?

In most cases, you will have more influence if you give it to a specific candidate. Money sent to a party rather than a candidate will be used as the party sees fit to support candidates who have strategic value for that party.

CAN I GIVE DONATIONS TO MORE THAN ONE CANDIDATE?

Yes, but there are restrictions. For the years 2023-2024, the federal election law states:

It is complicated. Be sure to research the details if you are planning gifts that are approaching the above limits. A helpful website for locating all the details is https://www.fec.gov/help-candidates-and-committees/candidate-taking-receipts/contribution-limits/

State and local election districts might have their own legal limits. It is best to consult with your city and state office of elections to determine what the boundaries, if any, are for your locale.

You can donate to multiple candidates if your donation is, at most, $3,300 per candidate.

CAN I GIVE TO A PRESIDENTIAL RACE, DOWN-BALLOT, OR ACROSS THE BOARD?

You can contribute to as many candidates as you desire if you stay within federal and local laws.

SHOULD I SEND MONEY TO INDIVIDUALS OUTSIDE MY DISTRICT TO SUPPORT CANDIDATES WHO HAVE A CHANCE TO UNSEAT INCUMBENTS WITH WHOM I DISAGREE?

It is legal to financially support a candidate who resides outside your voter jurisdiction. You are free to contribute to anyone you please financially. This action is permitted, which might be a wise strategy on a federal or state level.

HOW MUCH MONEY AM I ALLOWED TO GIVE?

For federal elections, see the chart **Can I give donations to more than one candidate?** above. For state and local elections, consult with your city and state office of elections to determine what the limits, if any, are for your locale.

CAN I DESIGNATE THAT MONEY GO TO A SPECIFIC CANDIDATE?

Yes, you can donate to a specific candidate.

CAN I VOLUNTEER MY TIME, AND WHOM DO I CONTACT TO VOLUNTEER TO HELP?

It is perfectly legal to volunteer your time.

There is no specific answer to how and where to volunteer your time. To determine what is best for you, consider:

- Your personal skill set;
- Your financial situation;
- How dedicated you are to a specific cause or candidate and
- Where can you have the most significant impact?

On local levels, most candidates' websites indicate an email address, contact number, or mailing address.

On the state level, contact the state political party to which the candidate belongs.

On a federal level, contact the closest national party headquarters in your locale.

CHAPTER 10

How U.S. Elections Work

Keywords: County, Fraud, States, Voter eligibility.

WHY DO WE NEED ELECTIONS?

It is in our genes to join groups following a leader or several leaders. The first leaders could defeat their rivals, were better hunters, had more charisma, or all of the above.

The matriarch, the oldest and wisest female elephant, almost always leads herds or parades of elephants. An alpha male dog leads packs of wolves. Herds of buffalo do everything their leader directs without question. When human hunters kill the leader, the rest of the group stands around immobilized and baffled. The result is that hunters can easily slaughter the whole herd.

Peter E. Tarlow and Stephen H. Vincent

Somewhere along the way, the leadership of a group became something that the leader handed down to their offspring. In many cases, the leader had so much power that others could not stop them from handing leadership power to one of his kin. It happened that a lot of relatives who became leaders were less capable than the previous leader. Consequently, people became dissatisfied or craved power for themselves, so they replaced—or killed, more often than not—the weak leader with someone else. When there was a change in leadership, people often chose a side, after which a war ensued, and lives and property were destroyed.

No one knows when people decided there must be a better way to choose a leader than destroying everyone and everything. We know that the ancient Greeks introduced a system of political changes called dēmokratiā, which means "rule by the people". It seems the Athenian Greeks chose their leaders by dropping a pebble into an urn marked with the name of their favorite candidate. Despite the tremendous political progress made by the Greeks, few other nations of the time followed their example.

Throughout history, most leaders earned their titles either by heredity or violence rather than by some form of a popular vote. In the 18th century, the United States reintroduced the concept of elections when the U.S. Constitution was adopted, specifying that the members of the House of Representatives were elected directly by the people.

WHAT ARE THE CHARACTERISTICS OF THE AMERICAN ELECTION SYSTEM?

The American people created the U.S. elections system to determine many answers to questions that reach into the essence of our being and touch on such important issues as life and death. Elections can significantly impact a nation's future and countless generations to come.

The United States held its first Presidential election in 1788–1789. George Washington won the election and became the nation's first president. Most American political scientists argue that regularly scheduled elections are the best way to choose a leader for several reasons:

- In a fair election, the candidates who champion the ideas most people support become the leaders.
- Leaders are encouraged to fulfill the will of the people.
- There is an orderly change in leadership.
- Fair, regularly scheduled elections mean no one person is a dictator for life, and this system helps keep the leader from passing the leadership along to their friends or family.

- Elections allow citizens to participate in the election process and have their thoughts and ideas heard.

HOW OFTEN DO WE HAVE ELECTIONS?

In the United States, we have several levels of government. We have the Federal government that influences all states and United States territories. Each state or territory also has its own government. There are county governments, municipal districts, and city and town governments. We even have school districts and homeowner associations. The answer to how often we have elections is any time and all the time.

For reasons of simplicity, we will focus primarily on the United States national elections.

In 1789, the first presidential election occured following the newly adopted Constitution. Only ten of the original thirteen colonies sent electors to select the first President of the United States. North Carolina and Rhode Island did not vote because, at the time, they had not ratified the Constitution, and New York chose not to send anyone. The electors chose George Washington as the first President of the United States.

WHEN ARE NATIONAL ELECTIONS HELD?

A federal law passed in 1845 established the second Tuesday after the first Monday in November as Federal Election Day. The date considered that the electors were to meet in December to cast their vote for President, and since most of the people were employed in agriculture, the election would not interfere with their jobs. Starting with the election of 1848, every four years, on the second Tuesday after the first Monday in November, we vote to elect the President (McNamara, 2019).

WHAT IS THE DIFFERENCE BETWEEN A PRIMARY ELECTION AND A GENERAL ELECTION?

Primary elections choose the candidate to represent a party in the general election. General elections choose the person who will serve in that specific position (office).

WHO CAN VOTE IN A PRIMARY ELECTION?

This answer depends on your state's laws. For the most part, it is any person who declares themselves to be part of that political party.

ARE ALL ELECTIONS HELD IN NOVEMBER?

Not necessarily. Local elections can be held at any time. Local districts, cities, counties, and states can choose when they have their elections. The local political entity's laws or governing body sets the dates of local elections.

WHAT OFFICES ARE ON THE BALLOT?

The election for president/vice president takes place every four years. On the ballot for national offices are the candidates for President of the United States, perhaps a United States Senator to represent your state, and a United States Representative for your congressional district. There might even be a proposed amendment to the United States Constitution if your state is voting to accept or reject such a proposed amendment.

Elections every four years are important since all these levels of government affect so much of our lives. Every four years, there is an opportunity to select leaders who can impact our lives.

We also have federal elections every two years after the presidential election. For this election, your ballot will include candidates for U.S. Senator representing your state if that office is part of the one-third of U.S. senators up for election. Why one-third? What about the other two-thirds of senators? The term of a United States senator is six years. So, over the course of ten years, two elections will have a ballot for a senator from your state, and there will be one election where there will be no election for U.S. Senator. In this one election in ten years, both U.S. Senators representing your state will not yet have completed their six-year term.

On the other hand, all candidates for the U. S. House of Representatives will be on the ballot since their terms are for two years.

There will be candidates for your state's governor, state representatives, local officials, and maybe proposed amendments to your state constitution. In all states and U.S. territories, governors serve for four years, except in Vermont and New Hampshire, where governors serve for two years. Remember that each state or government entity has its own Constitution or rules it follows.

WHAT OTHER OFFICEHOLDERS DO WE ELECT?

Cities, counties, and states are free to decide what offices are to be elected. Often, these include:

- Justice of the peace and other judges;
- Sheriffs;
- County commissioners;
- School board members and Heads of state commissions.

WHO IS ENTITLED TO VOTE?

Eligibility to vote in the United States is established through the United States Constitution and state law. With few exceptions, a U.S. citizen can vote as long as:

- They are a U.S. citizen;
- They meets a state's residency requirements, and
- They are 18 years old. Some states allow 17-year-olds to vote in primaries and register to vote if they are 18 before the general election.

Always check with the state where you live if you have questions. For example, almost every state has laws that do not allow people convicted of a felony or judged mentally incompetent by the state to vote for state offices. Some states allow you to vote in state elections after serving your sentence, and others do not let prisoners vote regardless of their crime.

WHAT IDENTIFICATION DO I NEED TO VOTE?

In many states, bringing your voter registration card or showing your assigned precinct (the building or location where voters cast their ballots) is helpful. Your legal voting residence determines the precinct.

In most places, a valid driver's license is sufficient once your name appears on the official voting registration. In all cases, it is best to check with local election officials.

States requiring photo IDs, such as a driver's license, are Alabama, Arkansas, Florida, Georgia, Idaho, Indiana, Kansas, Kentucky, Louisiana, Michigan, Mississippi, Missouri, Montana, New Hampshire, North Carolina, Ohio, Oklahoma, Rhode Island, South Carolina, South Dakota, Tennessee, Texas, and Wisconsin.

States in which some form of identification that does require a photo are Arizona, Colorado, Connecticut, Delaware, Iowa, North Dakota, Utah, West Virginia, and Wyoming.

Eighteen states that do not require identification are California, Hawaii, Illinois, Maine, Maryland, Massachusetts, Minnesota, Nebraska, Nevada, New Jersey,

New Mexico, New York, Oregon, Pennsylvania, Vermont, Virginia, Washington, and Washington, D.C (Voter identification laws by state, 2023).

WHAT TYPES OF VOTING MECHANISMS DO WE HAVE IN THE U.S.?

There are multiple voting methods. These go from simple paper ballots to mail-in voting. Each district uses the method it thinks best suits its needs.

Eight states conduct all-mail elections, where every eligible voter is mailed a ballot without requesting one. Ballots are returned through the mail or placed in secure ballot drop boxes or election offices.

In two states, in all elections, certain counties vote by mail.

Nine states allow mail-in voting for nonfederal elections that do not occur with regularly scheduled elections.

Four allow mail-in voting for small jurisdictions.

Twenty-eight states do not allow vote-by-mail elections except for absentee ballots.

WHAT ARE ABSENTEE, SPECIAL, OR EARLY VOTING BALLOTS, AND ARE THEY THE SAME?

If you cannot go to your assigned polling place on election day, you can apply for an absentee ballot. Depending on the state, valid excuses for absentee ballots can include preexisting work or school obligations, illness or infirmity, military service, or religious reasons. Most states also have early voting that allows citizens to vote for about a week before the election day. Early voting is open to all citizens, and no reason is necessary to participate.

If a person loses vision, they may want to vote absentee. Suppose the person is a senior citizen or disabled at election time and cannot get to the voting place. Your local voting office can provide you with the most current transportation or alternative information.

Voters with special needs can vote at home, *via* the Internet (in some states), or at polling stations with a trusted friend or relative. Many voting stations also have machines that can accommodate voters with special needs, such as vision.

Be sure to check with your state on their rules for voting absentees. An informative site is https://www.eac.gov/voters/register-and-vote-in-your-state

WHAT IS EARLY VOTING?

If your state allows early voting, it is a great way to vote in person when it is more convenient for you rather than spend a lot of time waiting in line on election day. Like almost everything else in the voting process, your state has its own rules. One state starts early voting forty-six days before the election, and most close from three days to one day before voting day. Some states do not allow early voting, but they usually allow absentee voting.

Get the details on early voting in your area from your local election office. You can find the answers to many of your questions about elections on a helpful website such as https://www.eac.gov/voters/register-and-vote-in-your-state.

IS THERE SUCH A THING AS A PROTEST VOTE?

Yes! It is your right to reject any and all candidates running for office! Write in a person you feel would make a good president. Write in Mickey Mouse or George Clooney. Another way is to stay at home if neither of the candidates is your favorite and did not win the primary. If you are so inclined, vote for all the other offices and leave it blank for the office where you do not like anyone.

Let us play with this for just a minute. Running for President of the United States is someone named Cheesecake, and Diamond Back Rattlesnake opposes Cheese.

One of Cheesecake's campaign promises was to make everyone eat at least one dessert daily. Diamond Back Rattlesnake campaigned to have all citizens put a rattlesnake in bed with them so snakes can be warm at night.

You are allergic to dairy products, so you cannot bring yourself to vote for Cheesecake. You live in the West and are familiar with rattlesnakes and what they can do. Many voters live in cold climates, do not have rattlesnakes around their homes, and think having another warm body in bed with them might be a good idea.

You listen to both candidates and decide neither candidate perfectly aligns with your views. You do not like this dessert issue and are logically scared of sleeping with a rattlesnake. You decide you cannot vote for either one, so you sulk and sit this one out, or you vote for George Washington.

After all the millions of votes were counted, Diamond Back Rattlesnake became the new President of the United States. So many dessert protestors did not vote that Cheesecake would have won if the dessert protesters had voted for him.

Three months later, there is a knock on your door, and someone gives you your new bed partner. Rattle, rattle. Still happy with your protest?

The best way to ensure there is a good candidate for you and the people of America is to get involved as soon as possible. No votes and protest votes are votes. Elections have consequences.

WHO COUNTS THE VOTES?

There are several methods for vote counting. In many locations, votes are counted and electronically reported by voting officials. If the vote is very close, a candidate can demand a recount. Each state has a specific definition of "a very close vote".

WHAT IS A RECOUNT, AND WHEN DO WE RECOUNT THE BALLOTS?

Each state has rules that define when a recount will take place and how it will be performed. A recount means taking a statistical sampling of the ballots or recounting all the ballots to ensure the correct vote count. Recounts can be started when only a small percentage of votes separates the candidates. A candidate or political party can also demand a recount if there is evidence of tampering, incorrect vote totals, missing ballots, or anything that causes the voters to suspect an unfair election.

For a recount to be granted, the candidates must agree to hold the recount, or a court must rule that a recount is called for to assure the accuracy of the elections. In some states, there is an automatic recount when the margin of difference between the two candidates is below a set statistical limit. In a tie vote, there is first a recount, and should the tie hold, a coin is flipped to determine the winner.

Recounts can be extended and drawn out with much drama, such as the 2000 Florida voting for President of the U.S.

HOW DO WE KNOW THE VOTE IS FAIRLY COUNTED?

Each party or candidate has poll watchers who certify that the votes have been fairly counted. After local tallies, traditionally, the results are taken to a central office by sworn law enforcement officers. New methods include electronic transmittal. These new methods are being scrutinized for accuracy and resistance to tampering. A candidate's poll watchers can contest votes or challenge the outcome if they believe the vote tally is unfair.

Ensuring all votes are accurately counted is always a hotly debated topic because the margin between the candidates' vote totals can be slim. The difference between Clinton and Trump was about 2.9 million votes in the 2016 presidential election out of about 200 million registered voters, or about one and one-half percent.

One of the issues dealing with vote counting accuracy is the effect of mail-in ballots. U.S. Election Assistance Commission and the Election Administration and Voting Surveys data indicates that for both the 2016 and 2018 elections, 16.4 million ballots sent to registered voters by mail went missing. In the 2018 election, about 42.4 million ballots were mailed to registered voters. Results state that more than 1 million were undeliverable, more than 430,000 were rejected, and nearly 10.5 million went missing (Miller, 2020).

WHAT IS ELECTION FRAUD?

Election fraud has been with humanity for as long as there have been elections. An intended election irregularity is another form of stealing. There are as many ways to commit election fraud as stars in the sky. As the world becomes more sophisticated, so do the methods used in election tampering.

Elections do not necessarily mean that the loser will leave power peacefully. There have always been rigged elections. This manipulation of the election process is "fraud".

Throughout history, rulers who oppressed their people have not allowed them to vote. But there have been many rulers who stayed in power by letting their people vote. Why don't the people vote out these cruel dictators? Because the dictators make sure who wins through election fraud. Election fraud, or tricking someone and doing something illegal, can and has occurred in the United States. One of the most famous election fraud arguments is about Lyndon B Johnson's suspicious victory in 1948 for the U.S. Senator of Texas.

After several days of recounts in a runoff election, Coke Stephenson led by more than 150 votes. Miraculously, 202 votes for Lyndon B. Johnson (LBJ) appeared in South Texas, giving LBJ an 87-vote victory out of almost one million votes. The last 202 names on the rolls in Box 13 from Alice, in Jim Wells County, were listed at the bottom of the list, written in a different color ink; the new names were listed in alphabetical order; the handwriting was identical; and some of the new voters claim they never voted. After the legal battles went to the Supreme Court of the United States, Johnson became the Senator (Balz, 1990).

This suspected election fraud case had enormous effects on our country's history. LBJ was Vice President when John Kennedy was assassinated, and LBJ became President. LBJ played a huge role in the escalation of the Vietnam War, civil rights, and gun control and created an explosion in the size and reach of the federal government. Unfortunately, election fraud has occurred throughout the United States. The above example demonstrates how concerned our elected officials must be in preventing election fraud.

Although election pollsters try their best to ensure accurate results, this has not always been the case.

When money or power is involved, some people will spend much time, effort, and money to win. Dishonest people tamper with elections by misinformation, intimidation, vote-buying, recording votes incorrectly, misleading/confusing ballot papers, voting when not qualified, voting more than once, voting where they are not a resident, incorrect recording of votes, misusing proxy votes, destruction/damaging of ballots, and tampering with electronic voting machines. A commonly used tampering technique is having others vote for dead people.

HOW DO WE PROTECT AGAINST FRAUD?

Governments protect against fraudulent elections by having voters register to vote.

State governments are supposed to verify the state voter registration rolls against official state records. At the polling place, poll workers will verify that each voter is listed on the registered voter rolls for that precinct.

For all citizens to know the elections are fair and honest, those responsible for our elections must be watchful for fraudulent efforts to affect the outcome.

Since states decide who qualifies to vote, it is not surprising the requirements differ. Voter ID requirements are a hotly debated topic. Those who support the required use of a photo ID argue that photo IDs help eliminate voter fraud. Twenty states require a photo ID, twelve require an ID with or without a photo, and sixteen states and the District of Columbia require no ID.

According to ID advocates, a photo ID makes it difficult for non-citizens to commit a crime by illegally voting. They also argue that the photo ID stops people from voting multiple times and even keeps "dead people" from voting. Proponents of the photo ID argue that without this provision, non-qualified voters could affect election outcomes. They contend that if you consider only the non-ID required states, which include California, New York, Pennsylvania, Illinois, and

Washington D.C., over forty percent of the members of the House of Representatives elections could be affected by non-qualified voters. The same would be true for these states' senators and governors.

Those who argue against voter IDs state that minorities, the poor, the sick, or the elderly can easily be disenfranchised and deprived of some right, privilege, or immunity if an ID is required to vote.

WHAT IS A POLL WORKER?

Poll workers are trained to answer questions and have the legal authority to resolve problems raised by poll watchers and voters. They are the judges, so to speak, at the polling precinct. If you have an interest in working at a poll, visit https://www.eac.gov/election-officials/poll-worker-resources-election-officials

WHAT IS A POLL WATCHER?

Poll watchers are specially trained professionals or volunteers whose job is to ensure that the voting and vote counting are accurate and honest. Their main job is to give the people who vote confidence that the election is fair. Different states have slight variations in the duties of a poll watcher. Poll watchers are identified and approved about two weeks before an election. Most states do not allow law enforcement officers or elected officials to watch the polls because the intent is to ensure no voter feels intimidated.

Another common practice is for each candidate to have one or more of their own poll watcher(s). Most states allow poll watchers to challenge voters by discussing the issue with the poll workers, but the poll watchers are not allowed to approach a voter directly. Another common rule is that poll watchers cannot take pictures or record audio inside the polling place.

WHAT IF SOMEONE INTIMIDATES OR THREATENS ME?

Every state has laws against voter intimidation. It is a federal crime to try to reduce the number of votes based on race, color, national origin, or religion. It is illegal for someone to question, challenge you, or photograph or film you if it is decided they were trying to keep you or others like you from exercising your right to vote. Also, no one can stop you from marking your ballot or getting help from the person of your choice.

If you feel intimidated, do not confront the individual(s) yourself, but talk to the poll workers. If that does not solve the problem, contact and report the issue to local or federal law enforcement officers as soon as possible.

Some helpful resources include the Justice Department's online form for filing election-related complaints; your local U.S. Attorney's Office, where a designated staffer can answer questions and field concerns on Election Day; and the Election Protection Program, run by the Lawyers Committee for Civil Rights, which has a helpful website, along with English (1-866-OUR-VOTE) and Spanish (1-888-VE-Y-VOTA) hotlines for asking questions or reporting Election Day concerns or problems.

HOW DO WE REMOVE A POLITICIAN FROM OFFICE?

The best way is to vote the person out of office the next time that s/he runs. If you do not want to wait for the next election, many locations have means to hold a recall vote in which the public can declare that this official has lost the public's confidence and should no longer hold office.

The federal Constitution and each state's Constitution spell out a particular method for removing its officeholders. In the case of the U.S. president, impeachment does not mean removal from office. It takes two-thirds of the senators to vote to remove a president (or a Supreme Court justice) from their office.

CHAPTER 11

CONCLUSION

This book's goals are threefold. Its first goal is to educate. We hope that by reading it, you have a better idea of the details, the "ins and outs" of the American political system, and the workings of the American government. This book is a helpful guide for U.S. citizens desiring a better understanding of our governmental system. For non-Americans, the book will enlighten those who seek to understand the essence of the United States' political system.

The book's second goal is to help American citizens make wise choices when they vote. As such, this book encourages its readers to do their own research and to determine which candidates they support based not on emotions but facts. As part of one's research, we encourage our readers to have a non-emotional discussion with friends and family and share what they have learned. Really listen to their thoughts and opinions. Ask questions about the reasons behind your family and friends' ideas rather than always advocating for your own. There is an old saying that we have two ears and one mouth because we should listen twice as much as we speak. Do not be afraid to listen. Listening allows us to hear the other side and prevents emotions from overtaking reality. We are not electing a friend but leaders who can develop and implement policies that will serve us all now and in the future.

ACTIONS *VS* WORDS

The book's third goal is to help readers discern the differences between words and actions. Morality is not about what our politicians say but what they do. In times of great emotional and political turmoil, such as the current cycle, we must remember that our words and actions have consequences. When we seek to harm others with whom we disagree, we have chosen not only to disrespect one of the foundations of our country's Judeo/Christian ethic but also to destroy civil discourse and society.

Remember that politics is not a contact sport! The idea should be to pick the best people no matter which "team" the candidate is on! This book hopes that upon reading it, you, the voters, will agree that good leaders are essential. We should focus less on the personality of who wins an election, and instead, our concern should be about who can best serve the American people. Ultimately, our country will be better served if we devalue the quality of a leader's rhetoric and value the ideas a leader proposes more. The Biblical text teaches us that Moses successfully led the Israelites through the desert for over forty years. He was not an orator, but despite his lack of talent as a speaker, few would doubt that Moses was a great leader.

CHAPTER 12

The Practical Side for American Citizens

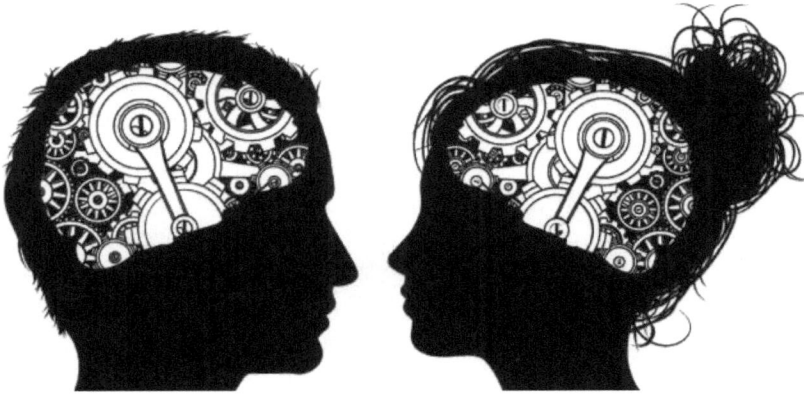

How you participate in the American system is a personal decision allowed by freedom in the United States. One narrow area is how do you, the American voter, decide for whom to vote. What ideals and ideas do you value enough to support? What ordinances or amendments do you favor? Before you vote, a little inventory of your beliefs, views, and requirements helps you cast an intelligent vote. What do you need, want, and expect from your elected officials?

To help you decide your priorities, we offer these exercises. There are no right or wrong answers. Think deeply about these questions and then vote your conscience. Remember, no one has a monopoly on truth. After studying the issues, each person must do what is right in their eyes.

First, take some time to think about these broad political-philosophical issues and then apply your thoughts to the specific subjects mentioned immediately after them. This book does not intend to tell you, the reader, whom to vote for or what propositions to support. The book's purpose is to inspire readers to contemplate the issues and candidates of the upcoming elections. Decide what is best for you, the reader, and for our country. How you vote will determine our immediate future and possibly the course of our national destiny for years to come.

Then, go back into American history and try to understand the nation's founders' ideas and goals. Many scholars and historians believe that our nation's founders felt local governments best served the needs of the citizens. Our founders wrote the Federalist Papers to explain the truths, principles, and logic of the proposed U.S. Constitution. The Papers indicate that our founders feared large bureaucracies and wanted the least political possible distance between the governed and those governing. For this reason, they stated that all powers not explicitly assigned to the federal government were to belong to the states. Do you agree with our founders? Do local governments best understand citizens' rights and needs?

At the beginning of the third decade of the twenty-first century, the world suffered from its greatest pandemic and the political consequences of COVID-19. From the American perspective, the COVID-19 crisis highlighted issues with the Bill of Rights (first ten amendments). It forced all of us to ask questions such as: At what point can the government withdraw our rights to freedom of assembly, freedom of worship, and freedom to work? Looking back, we must decide whether we answered these questions correctly or failed. How we analyze the COVID-19 years will have much to teach us about handling future crises.

To help you determine what decisions you can make, we offer a series of exercises and mental experiments. There are no correct answers. Instead, we encourage you to think about your answers and then determine what you, as an informed voter, think about the future of our country.

MENTAL EXPERIMENTS

Albert Einstein conducted mental experiments in his head as he walked the streets of Princeton, New Jersey.

None of us are Albert Einstein, but we can conduct a mental experiment no matter who we are. Please take a few moments to think about these questions, and then take a walk and try to answer them as you walk.

1. Assuming you are a delegate to a national presidential convention, what would you include in your party's platform? What would you want to exclude?

2. How do you make decisions? What outside influences do you have? Ask yourself, are you guided by nothing more than your whims, a religious text, what you read in the media, or some other inner or outer source?

3. Assume you are the President of the U.S. or the governor of your state and must conduct a news conference with many hostile media reporters:

How would you handle the news conference? What tone would you use with people who ask only "gotcha" questions?

4. Assume that you are the President of the United States and told that there is an illness abroad that might come to the United States but is not contagious: what would you say to the media?

5. Now assume that the Center for Disease Control gave inaccurate information: What would you do? What actions would you take?

6. Design a healthcare system. What would you include? How would you pay for it? What unexpected consequences might your system produce?

7. Imagine that you are running for a national political office. What would your platform be regarding domestic and foreign policy? What would be your top five priorities? How would you pay for your ideas?

True or false, or I do not know

Answer the following true-false statements to help determine what you believe or not believe regarding American politics.

8. A strong central government works best for the U.S.

9. The U.S. has been a successful country due to federalism and limited government.

10. I believe the U.S. media and journalists accurately report the news.

11. The U.S. Constitution permits most people to live a free and successful life.

12. The U.S. should copy European countries and their healthcare system.

13. Excessively taxing major corporations will force them to move outside the U.S.

14. It is a mistake not to produce essential products such as food, energy, or medicines at home.

15. Most politicians are more interested in themselves than the nation's welfare.

16. Anyone earning over $100,000 a year is rich.

17. Universities need to do a better job of preparing our young people to be good citizens.

TABLES

To help you make thoughtful decisions about these and other issues, we provide you with the following worktables to fill out privately. How you fill out these worksheets will help you determine how you will vote to guide the future of our nation.

Table 1. What sources are important for me to use in determining what is important?

Source	Rank	Comments
Religious text	-	-
Newspapers	-	-
Television/Radio	-	-
Media	-	-
The Internet	-	-
Personal research	-	-
Comments from friends and family	-	-

Table 2. What are the reasons you support a candidate? Please score each reason from 1 to 5, with 1 being the least and 5 being the most.

Reason for my support	Rank	Comments
Religious affiliation	-	-
Member of same ethnic group	-	-
Gender	-	-
Agree with the candidate's policies	-	-
Good speaker	-	-
Other	-	-

Table 3. Which qualities do you look for in a candidate? Please score each reason from 1 to 5, with 1 being the least and 5 being the most.

Quality	Rank	Comments
Is the right age to be President	-	-
Our country is safe and secure with this President	-	-
Is result-oriented	-	-
Good communicator	-	-
I share the candidate's moral positions	-	-
Is good looking	-	-
Is honest	-	-
Is consistent when stating their policies	-	-
Is pragmatic	-	-
Other	-	-

Table 4. Is there a domestic political issue that is a deal-breaker for you? Please score each reason from 1 to 5, with 1 being the least and 5 being the most.

Position	Rank	Comments
Regarding abortion or pro-life	-	-
A strong American military	-	-
Lower taxes	-	-
Climate change	-	-
Secure U.S. borders	-	-
Immigration	-	-
Healthcare reform	-	-
Other	-	-

Try not to allow politicians to distract you with emotional issues that have negligible impact. For example, ask yourself if educating our children to have the skills they will need to thrive in the coming decades or to worry about a celebrity's opinion is more important. Diving still deeper, what things are essential to help us as a nation thrive? Remember, you are not electing a friend but someone to run your community, state, or country.

After you have informed yourself on international and national issues and listened to the candidates talk about what they will do if elected, you are ready to make decisions. For many people, the next step will be to get involved in helping their chosen candidates win the election.

Table 5. Which international issues are most important to you? Prioritize from 1 to 5, with 1 being the least important and 5 being the most important.

Position	Rank	Comments
Support for NATO	-	-
Withdraw from NATO	-	-
Be tougher on China	-	-
Be tougher on Russia	-	-
Be tougher on Iran	-	-
Prevent nations such as Iran and North Korea from obtaining atomic weapons	-	-
Be supportive of traditional U.S. allies	-	-
Seek to solve Middle East conflicts	-	-
Support Ukraine	-	-

Table 6. Which nations are our best allies? Rank each one from 1–10.

Nation	Rank	Comments
Australia	-	-
Canada	-	-
France	-	-
Germany	-	-
Israel	-	-
Mexico	-	-
United Kingdom (England, Scotland, Wales, and Northern Ireland)	-	-
Spain	-	-
Japan	-	-
Ukraine		

Even if you are unhappy when the votes are counted, accept the results of a lawful election. If you support your chosen candidates, you will be satisfied with having done your part. Vow to continue to espouse your ideas lawfully in future elections. You will be a survivor.

From this book, we hope you have learned more about the government system in the United States and, if you are a citizen, are inspired to participate in the election process. Now, it is time to help shape the future of our great country, the United States.

Table 7. What foreign policy issues do you see on the horizon? Prioritize from 1 to 5, with 1 being the least important and 5 being the most important. Which are most important to you?

Issue	Rank	Comments
Reverse inflation	-	-
Contain China	-	-
Contain Russia		
End illegal immigration	-	-
Protect the environment	-	-
Reorient U.S. foreign policy away from Europe and pay more attention to developing nations in Africa and Asia	-	-
Stop nuclear proliferation	-	-
Stop acts of terrorism	-	-

BIBLIOGRAPHY

American Community Survey: 2011–2015. (2016, December 08). Retrieved from United States Census Bureau: .https://www.census.gov/newsroom/press-releases/2016/cb16-210.html

Balz, D. (1990). *The Mystery of Ballot Box 13.* Retrieved from The Washington Post: . https://www.washingtonpost.com/archive/entertainment/books/1990/03/04/the-mystery-of-ballot-box-13/70206359-8543-48e3-9ce2-f3c4fdf6da3d/

CFI. (2023) How the Government Makes Money. Retrievedfrom: . https://corporatefinanceinstitute.com/resources/economics/how-the-government-makes-money/

C-SPAN. (2019, September 2). *Retrieved from User Clip: Ted Cruz Questions Robert Epstein About Big Tech Election Interference:* .span.org/video/?c4814811/user-clip-ted-cruz-questions-robert-ep-stein-big-tech-election-interference

Retrieved from JSTOR Daily: .https://daily.jstor.org/the-unacknowledged-origins-of-the-deep-state/

Federal Workforce Statistics Sources: OPM and OMB (2022, June28). Retrieved from Congressional Research Services: .https://sgp.fas.org/crs/misc/R43590.pdf

Ken Drexler, R.S. (2021). *Constitution of the United States: Primary Documents in American History.* Retrieved from Library of Congress:.https://guides.loc.gov/constitution/introduction

40% of households will pay no federal income tax this year. Why that's good news. .

Retrieved from MarketWatch: https://www.marketwatch.com/story/40-of-households-will-pay-no-federal-income-tax-this-year-why-thats-good-news-11667240335.

McCarthy, J. (2020). *New High of 90% of Americans Satisfied With.* Retrieved from Gallup: .https://news.gallup.com/poll/284285/

McNamara, R. (2019). *Why Is Election Day on a Tuesday in November?*.thoughtco.com/why-is-election-day-on-a-tuesday-1773941

What do SCOTUS, POTUS, and FLOTUS mean? Retrieved from Merriam-Webster: .What do SCOTUS, POTUS, and FLOTUS mean?.https://www.merriam-webster.com/words-at-play/sco-tus-potus-flotus

Miller, A.M. (2020). *More than 16M mail-in ballots went missing from 2016 and 2018 elections: Re-port.* https://www.washingtonexaminer.com/news/more-than-16-million-mail-in-ballots-went-missing-from-2016-and-2018-elections-report

*National Archives. (2023, July 6). Electoral College. Retrieved from National Archives: .Electoral College.*https://www.archives.gov/electoral-college/about

U. S. Citizenship and Immigration Services Citizenship Rights and Responsibilities. (2020, July 5) Should I Consider U.S. Citizenship Retrieved from U. S. Citizenship and Immigration Services: .https://www.uscis.gov/citizenship/learners/citizenship-rights-and-responsibilities

Vote By Mail States. (2023, August) Retrieved from Vote by Mail: .https://worldpopulationreview.com/state-rankings/vote-by-mail-states

Voter identification laws by state. (2023). Retrieved from ballotpedia: . https://ballotpedia.org/Voter_identification_laws_by_state

We, the people of the United States, in order to form a more perfect union... (n.d.). https://www.archives.gov/founding-docs/constitution

SUBJECT INDEX

W

www.ingramcontent.com/pod-product-compliance
Lightning Source LLC
Chambersburg PA
CBHW060809270326
41928CB00002B/36